I0481603

2019

COLORING BOOK FOR KIDS

Copyright © 2018

All rights reserved.

ISBN: 1724444476

ISBN-13: 978-1724444479

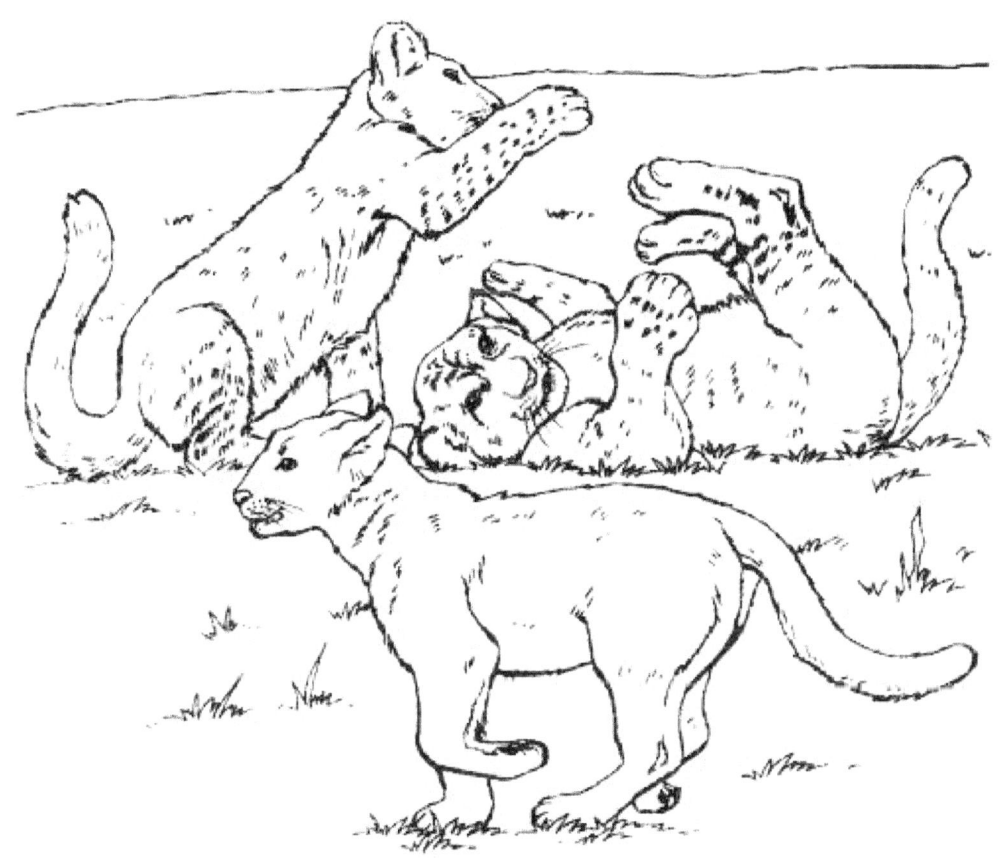

Lions

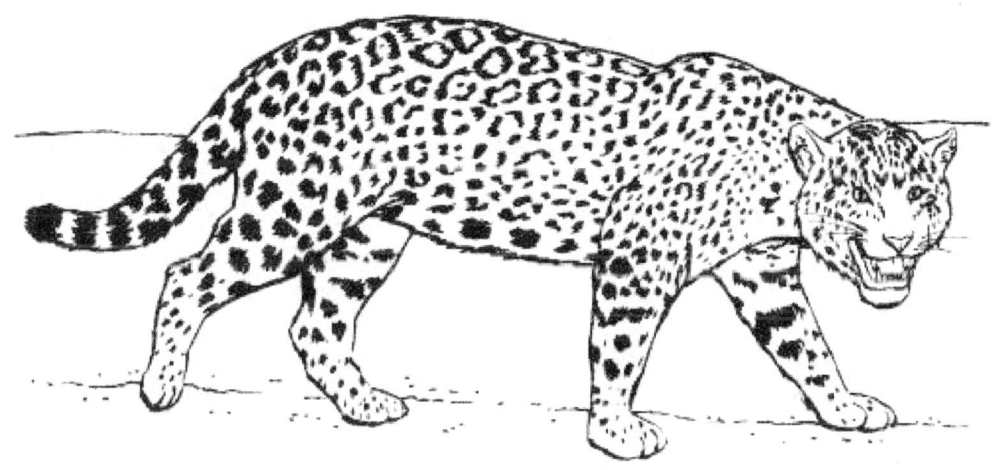

Jaguar

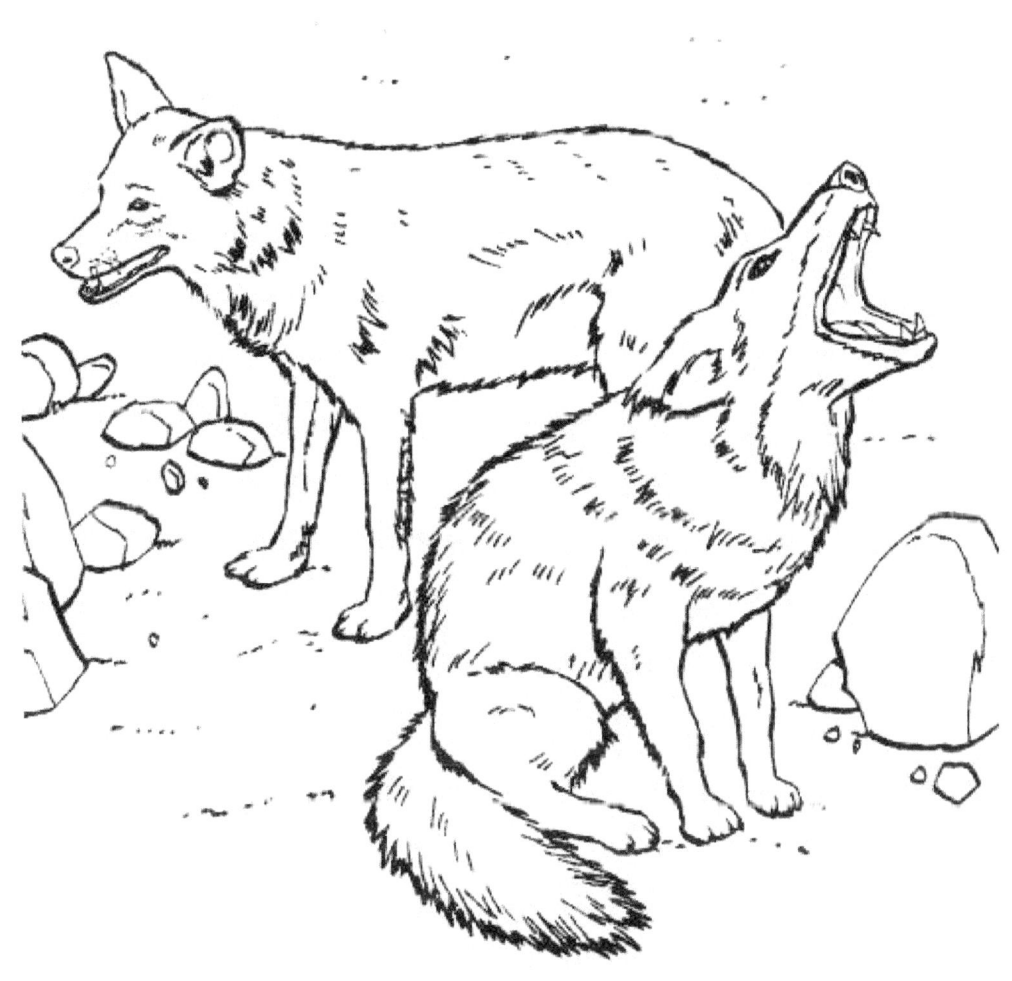

Coyotes are spread across
Alaska, Canada, USA, Mexico,
and Central America.

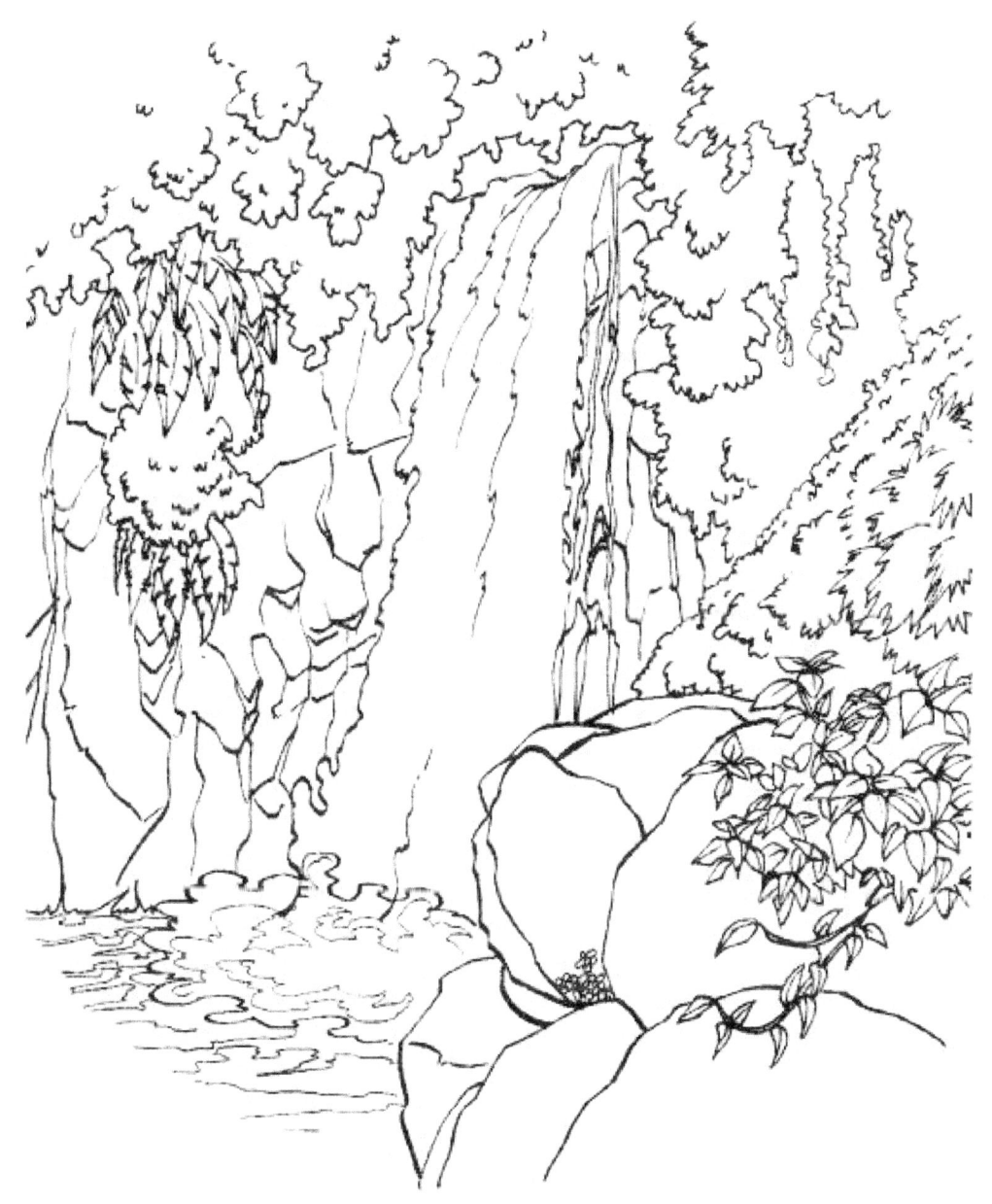

Waterfalls

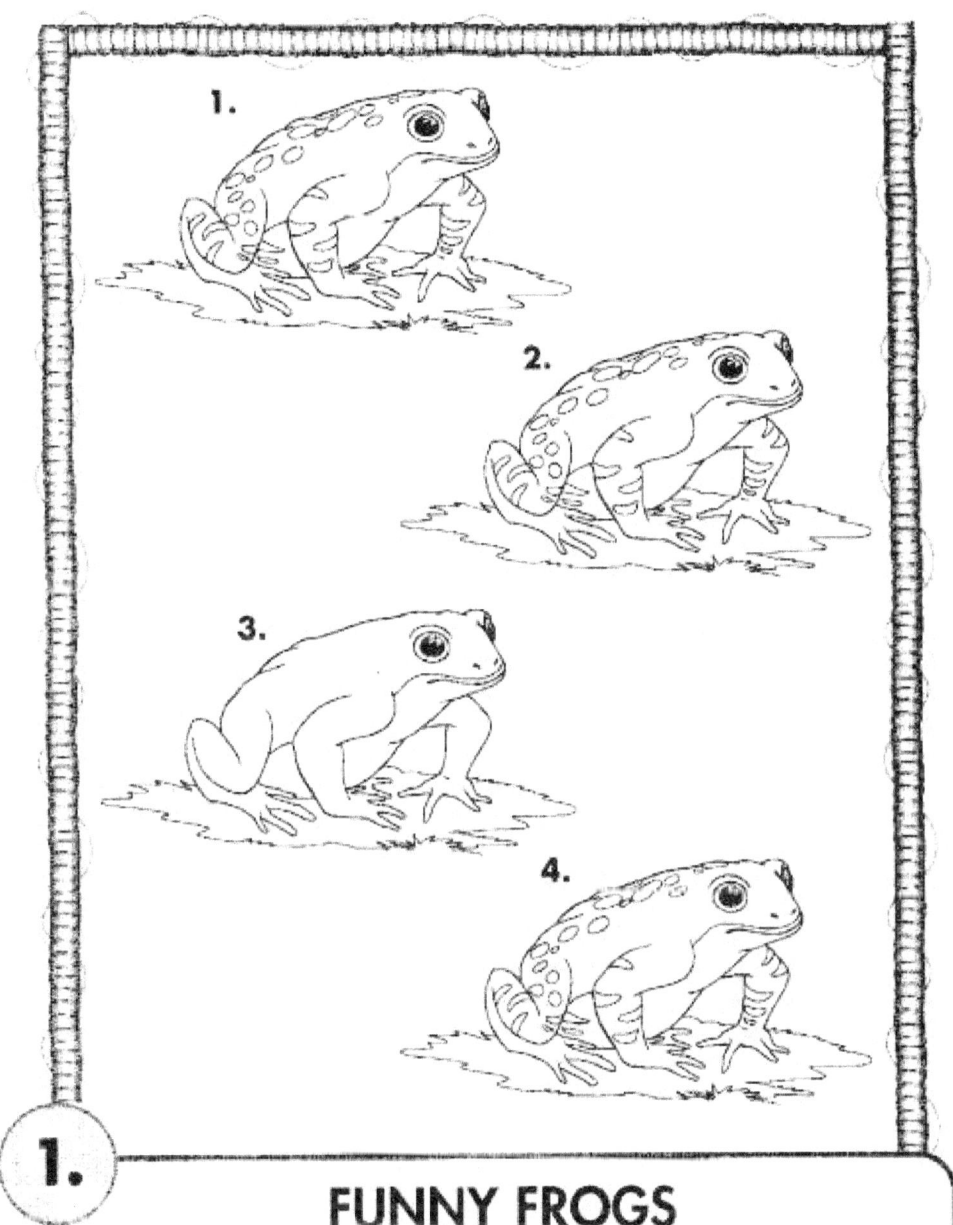

1.

FUNNY FROGS

One of these frogs is different from the others.
Circle him!

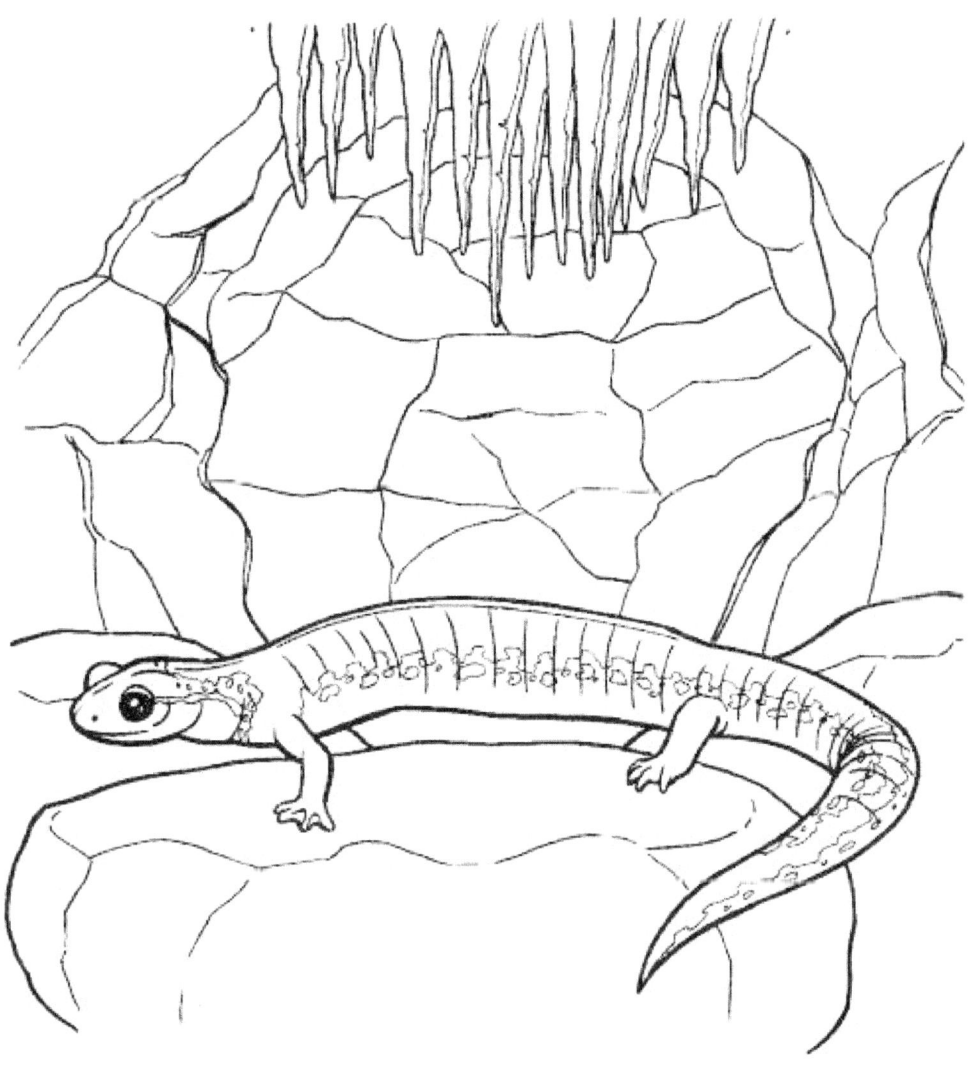

The cave salamander is able
to survive for up to 6 years
without food.

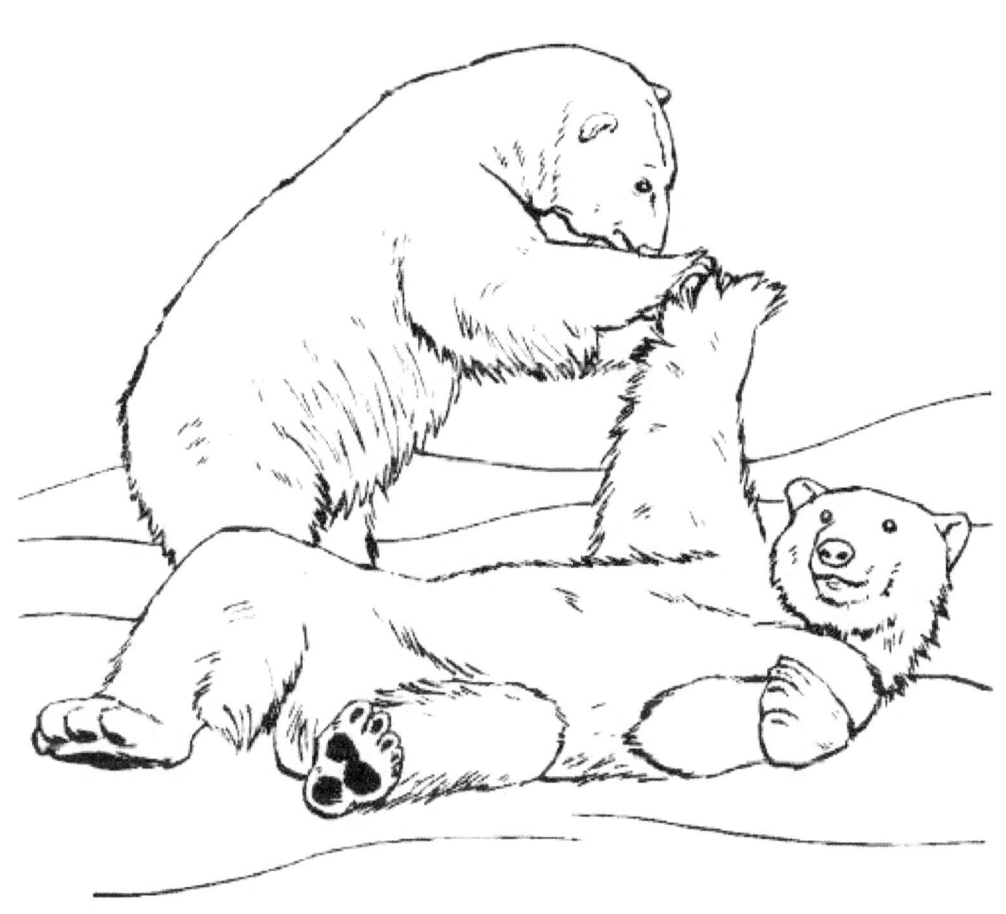

Polar Bears

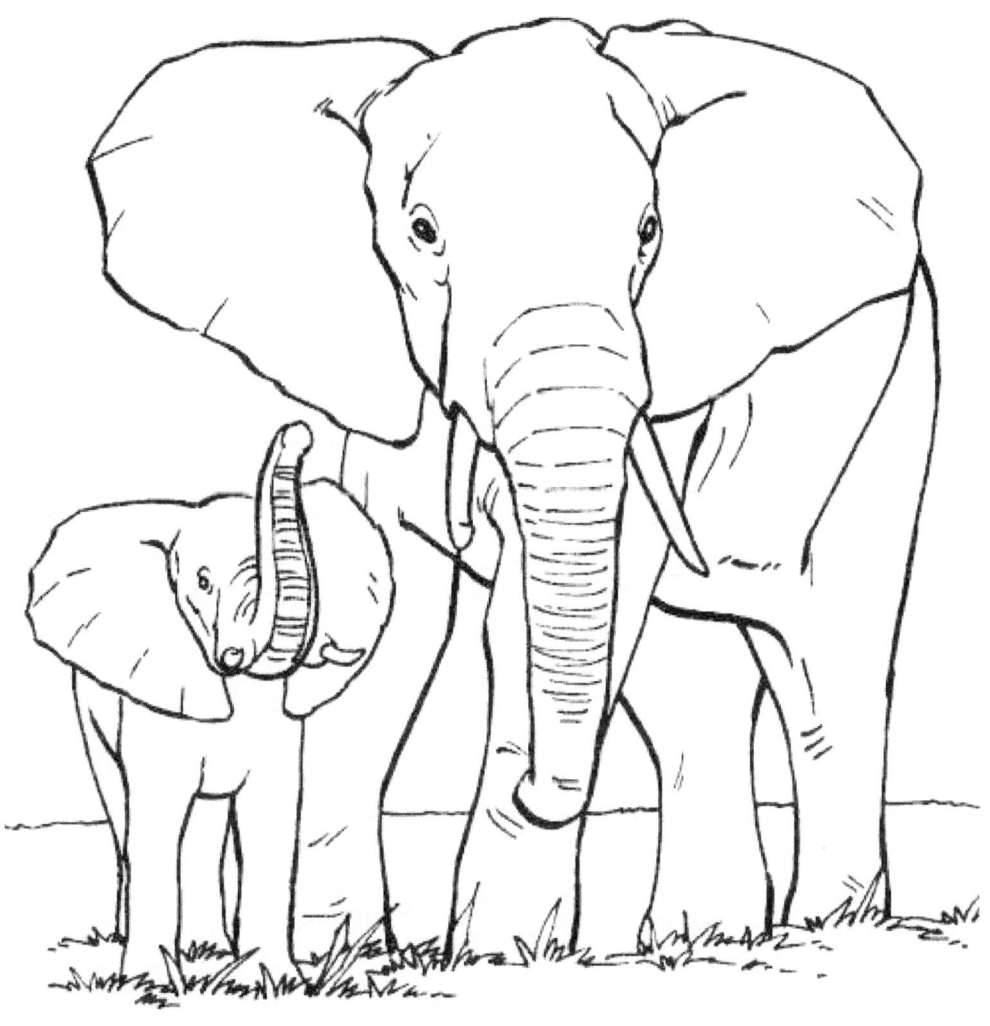

Elephants' ears are so big to
help keep them cool.

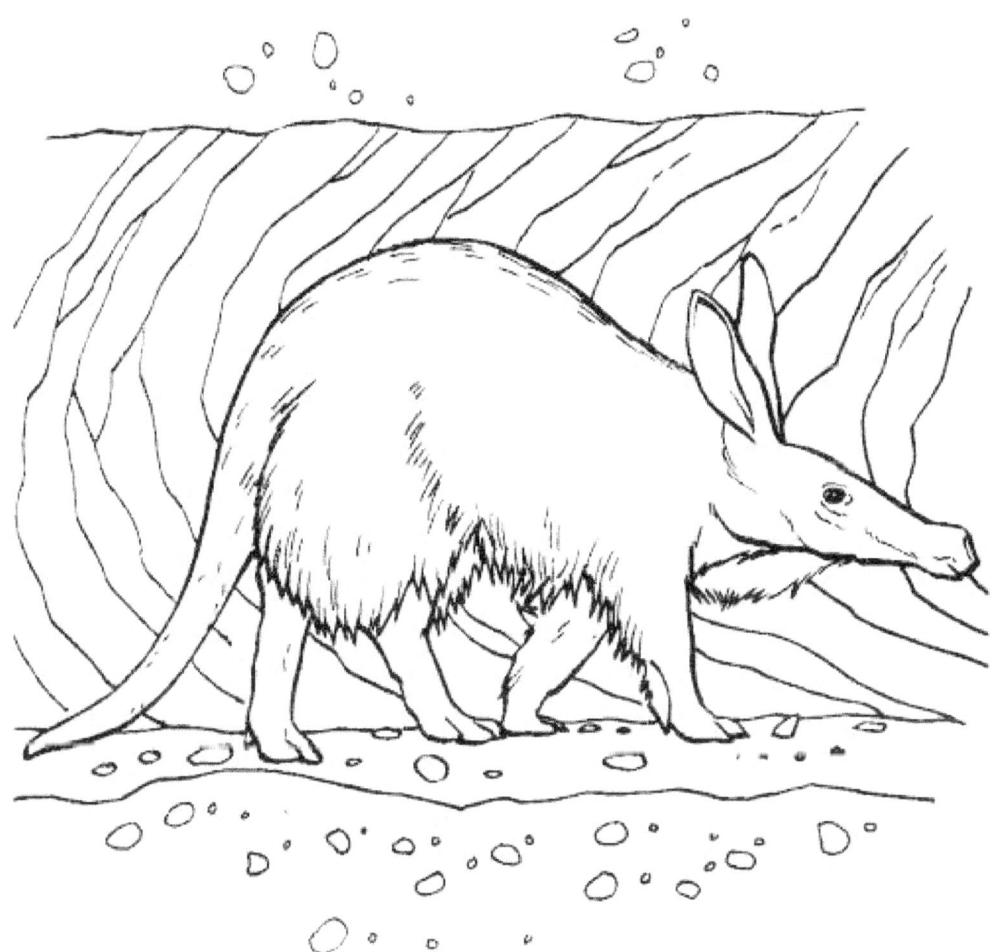

Aardvark

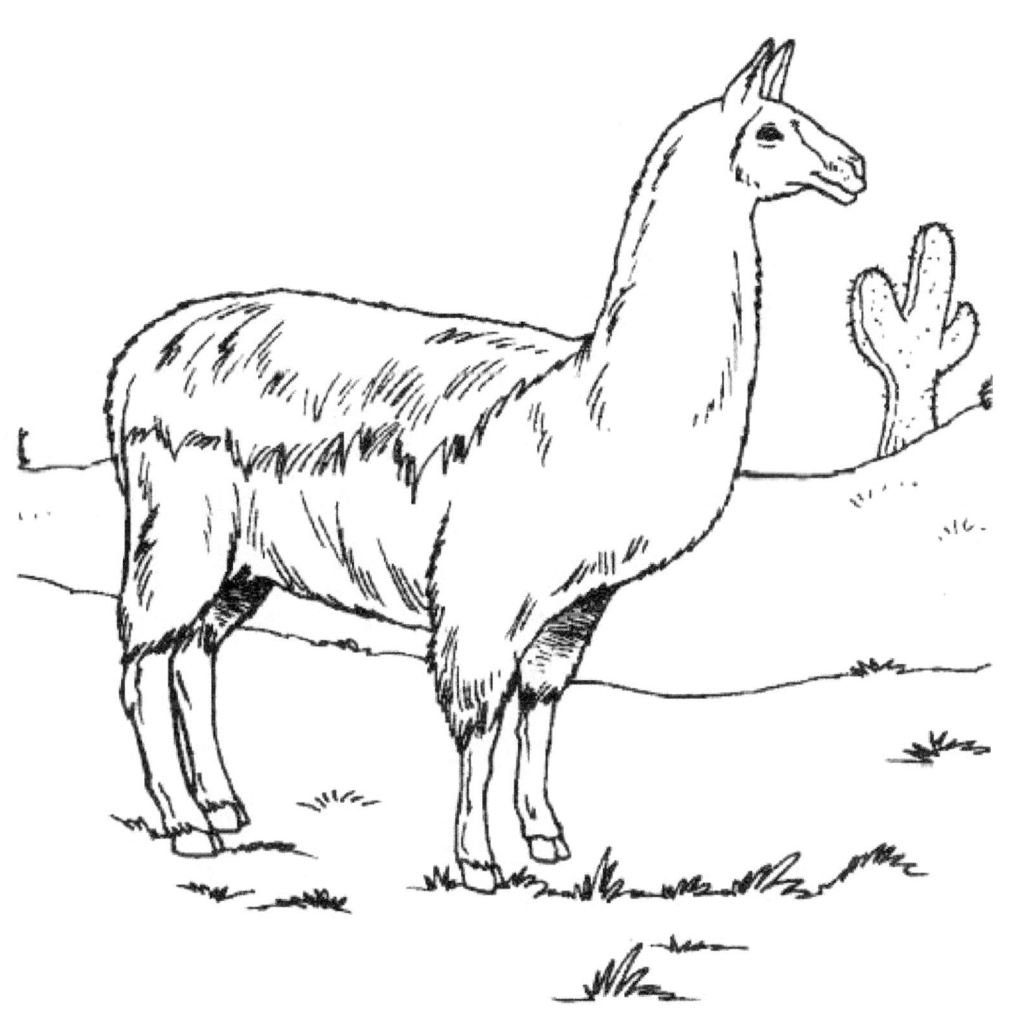

Llama

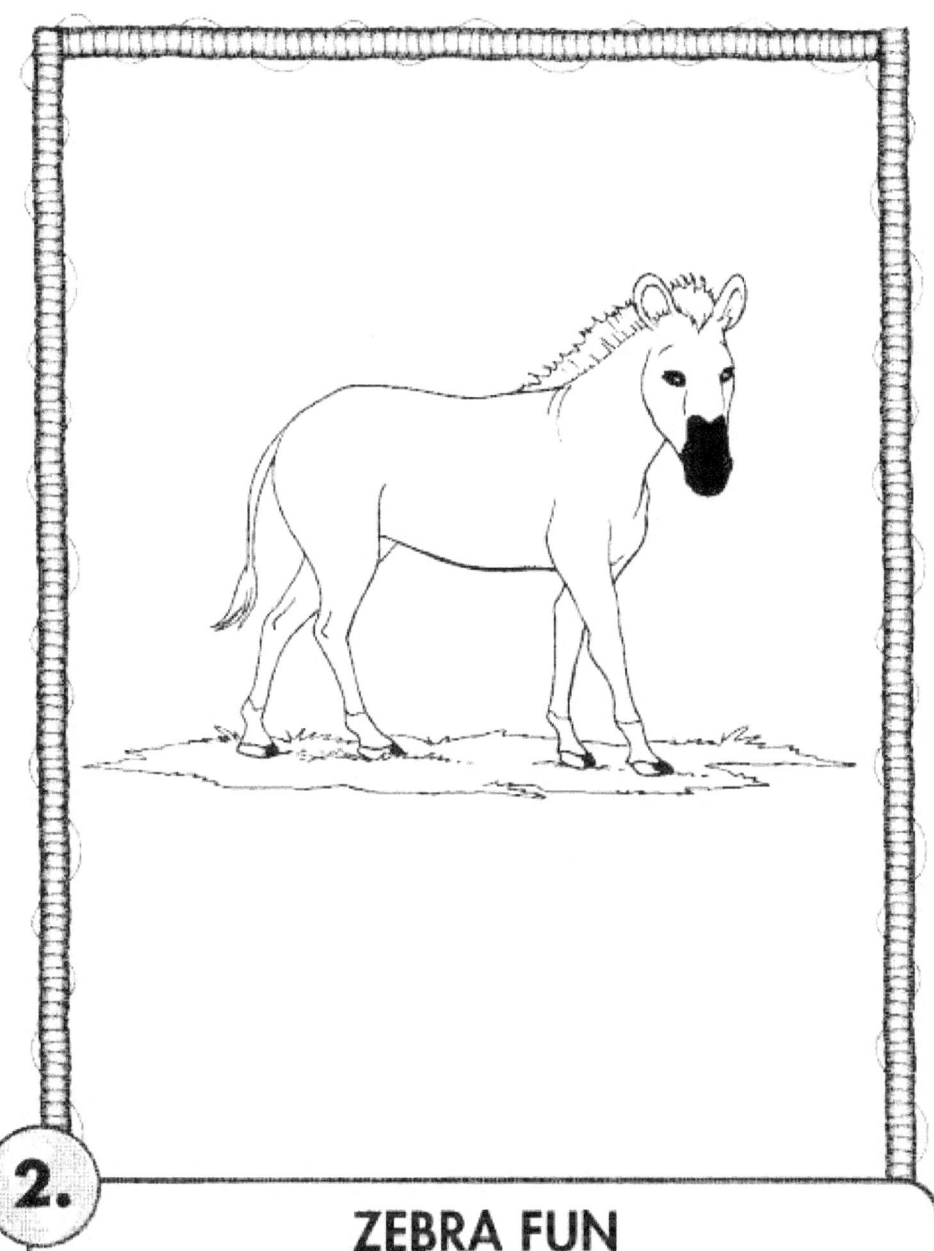

2.

ZEBRA FUN

This zebra is missing his stripes! Draw some stripes on him and be creative!

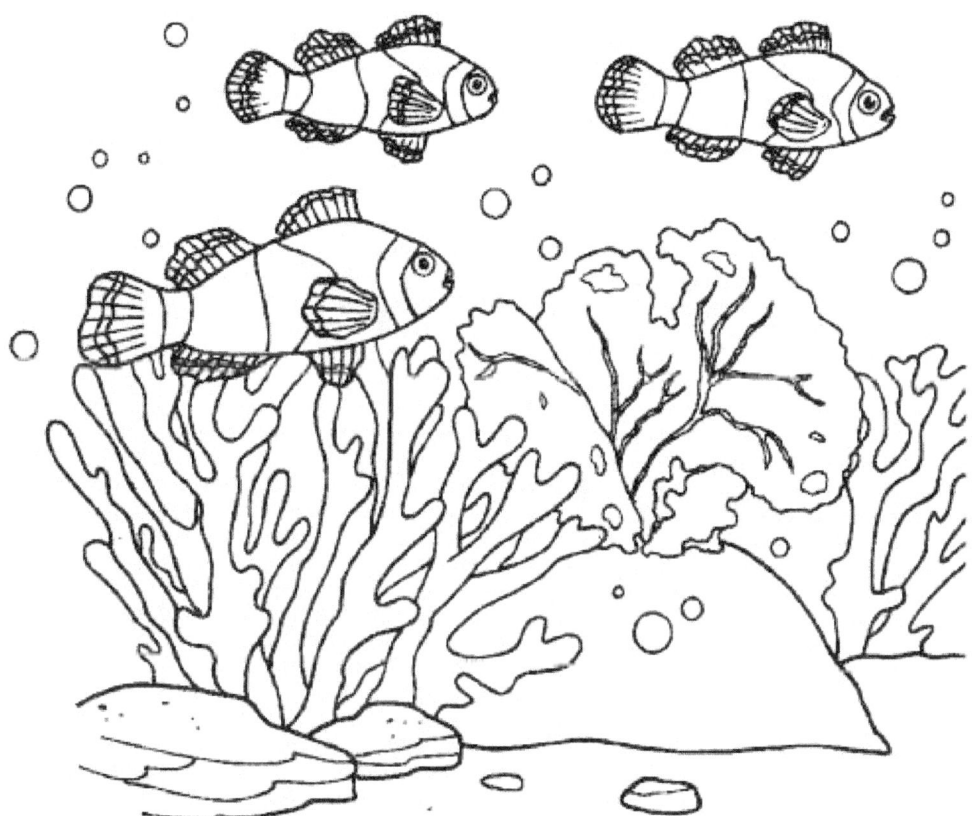

Clownfish

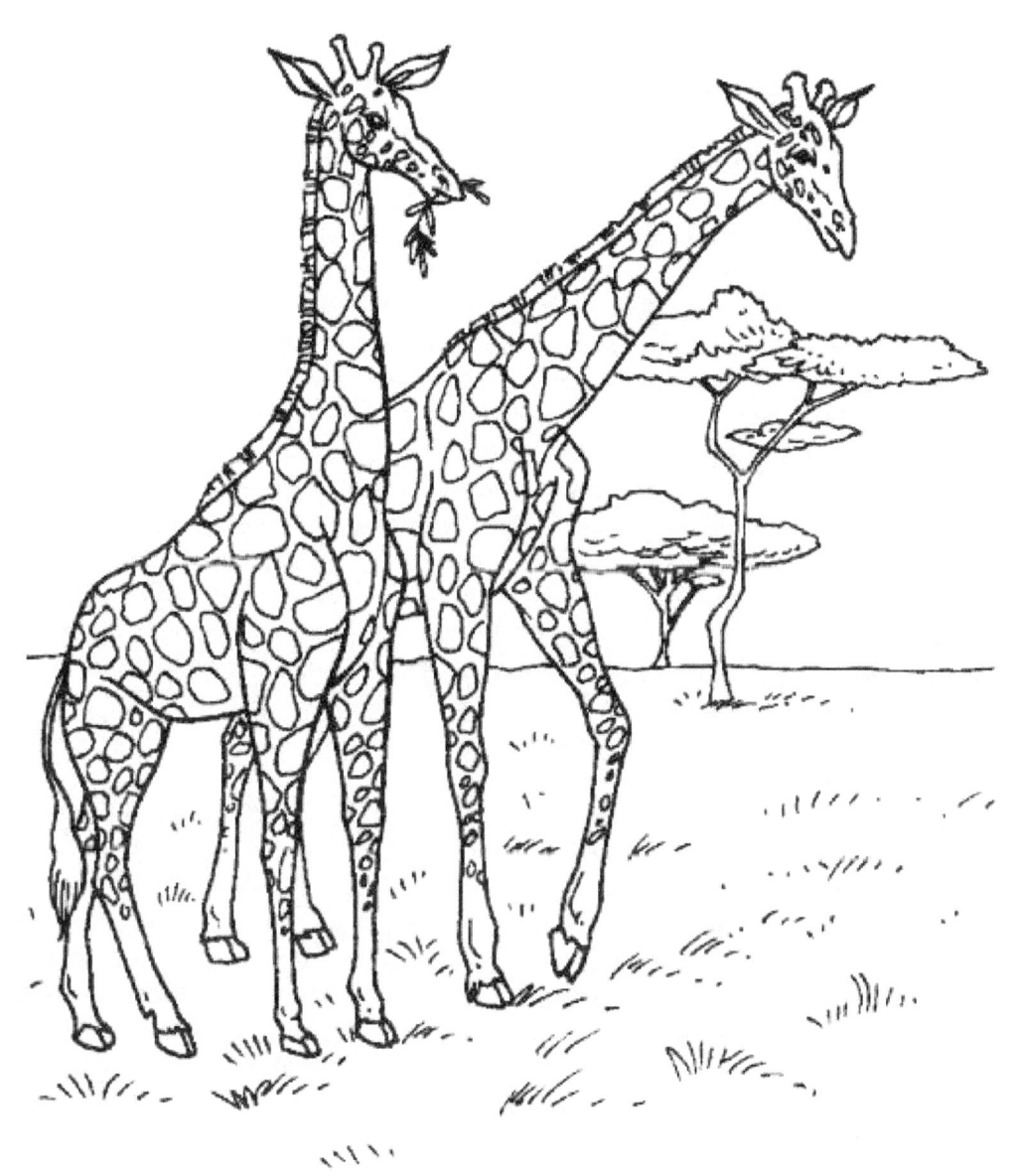

Giraffes

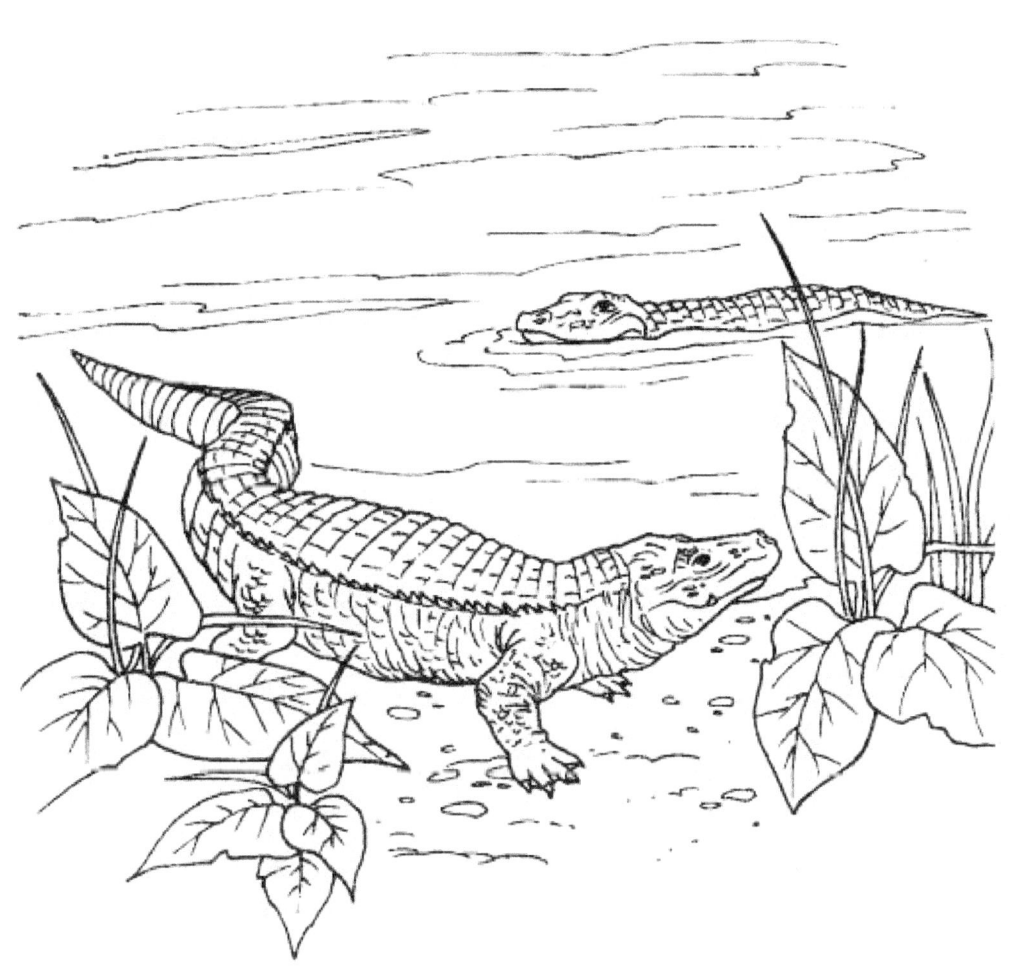

Alligators

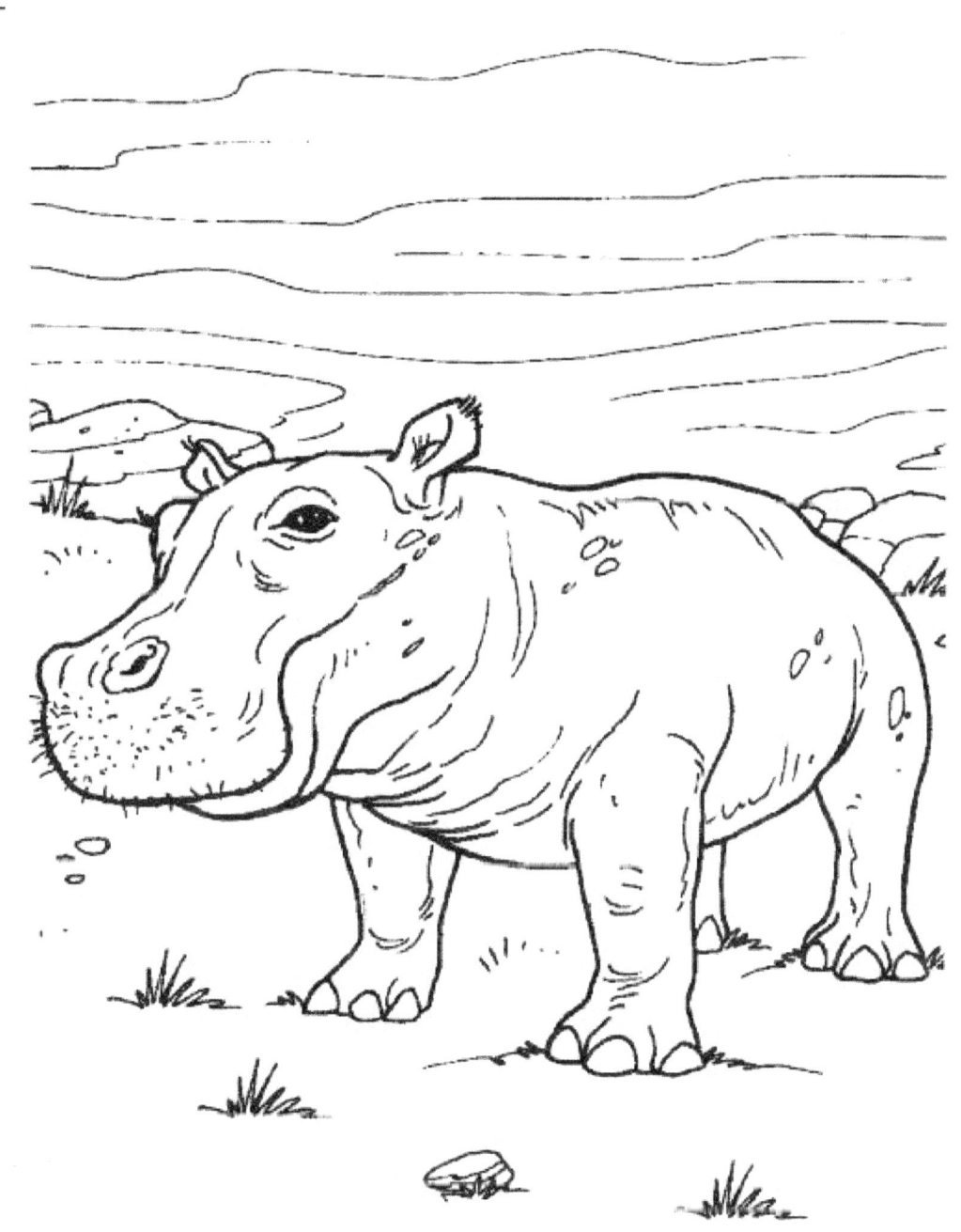

Hippopotamus

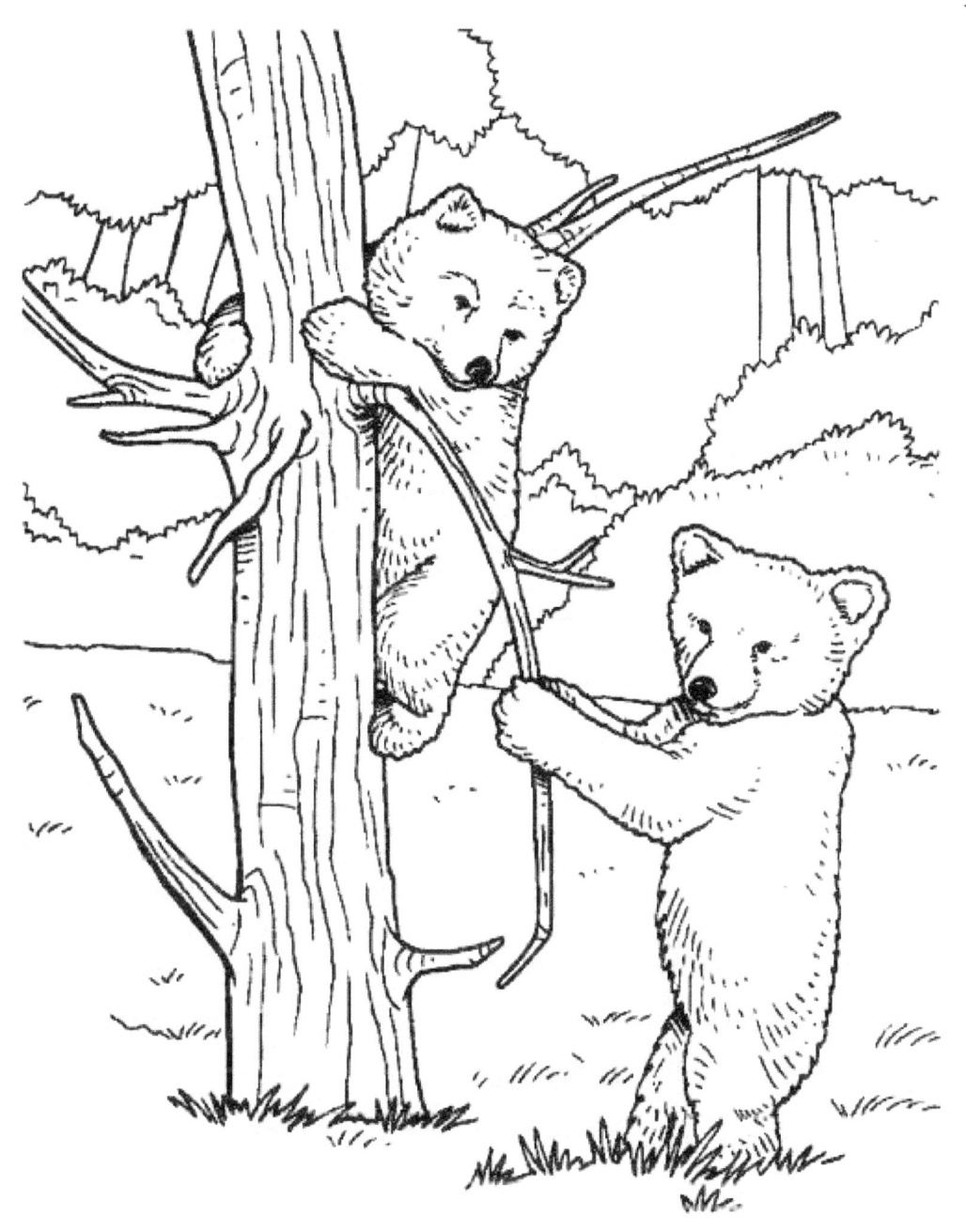

Bear Cubs

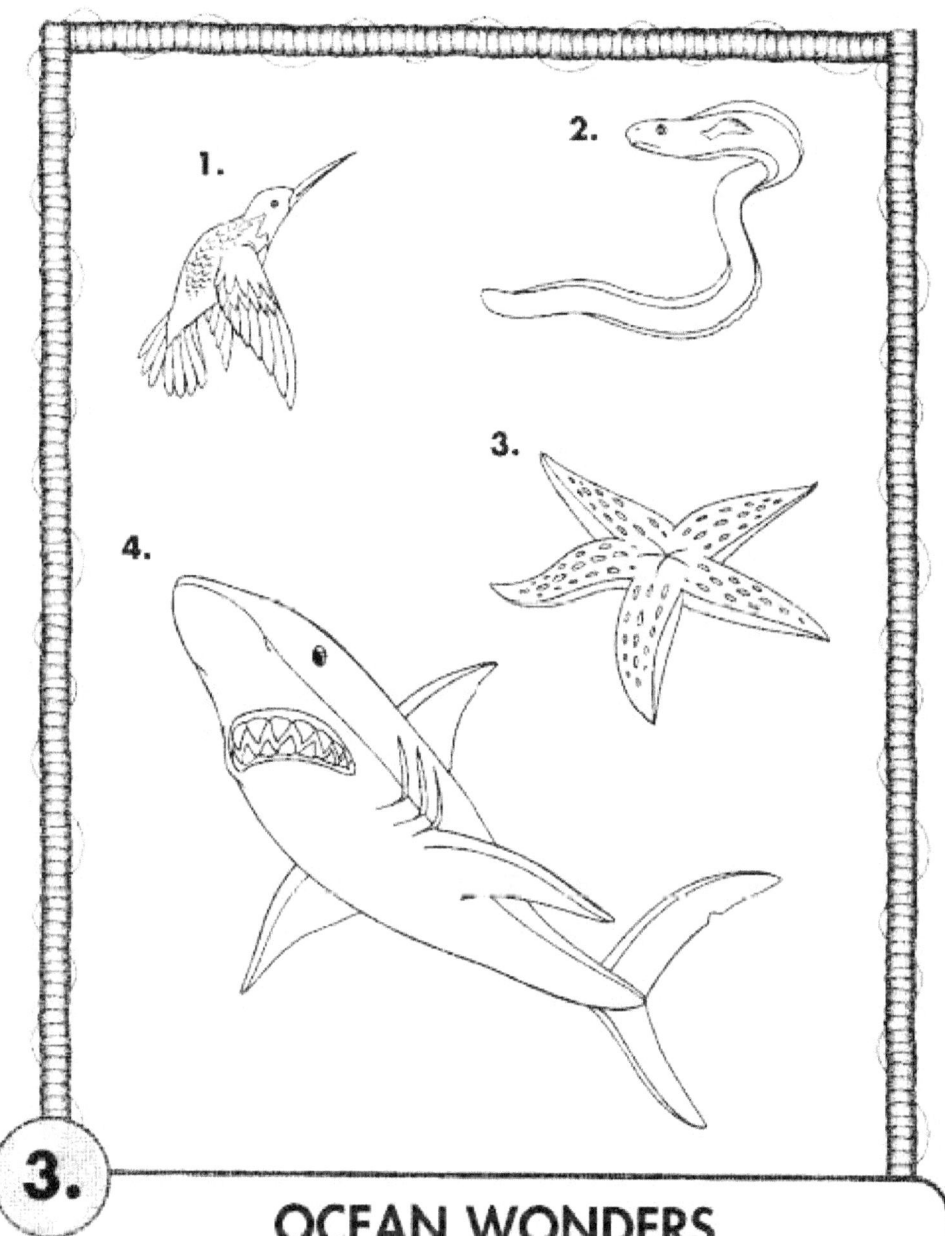

1.

2.

3.

4.

OCEAN WONDERS

Which animal would you not find in the ocean? Circle it!

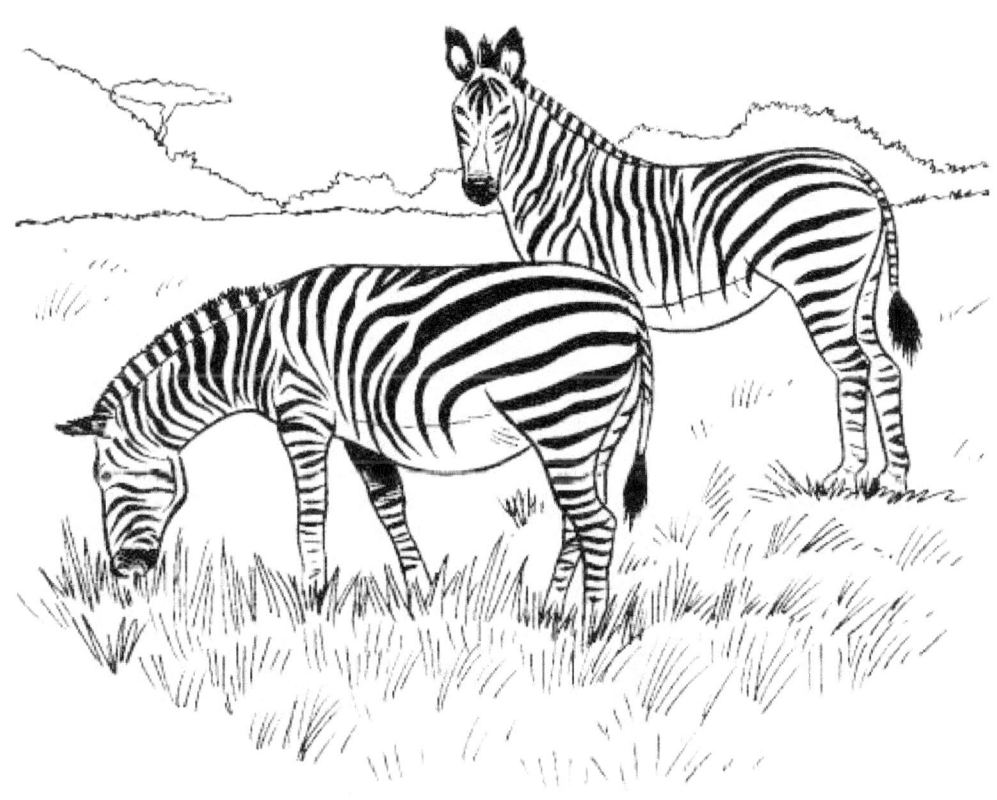

No two stripe coats on zebras are the
same – just like our fingerprints!

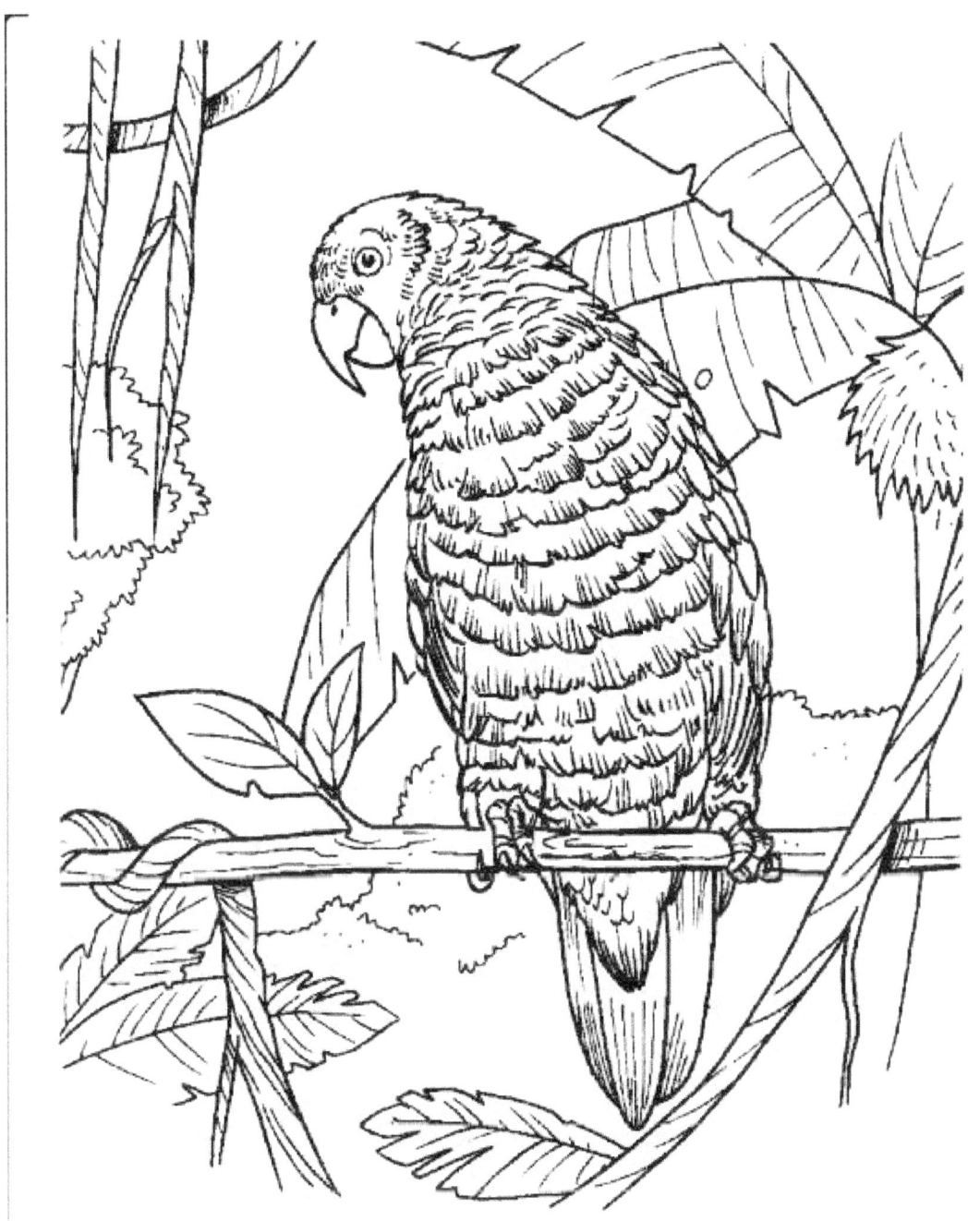

Parrot

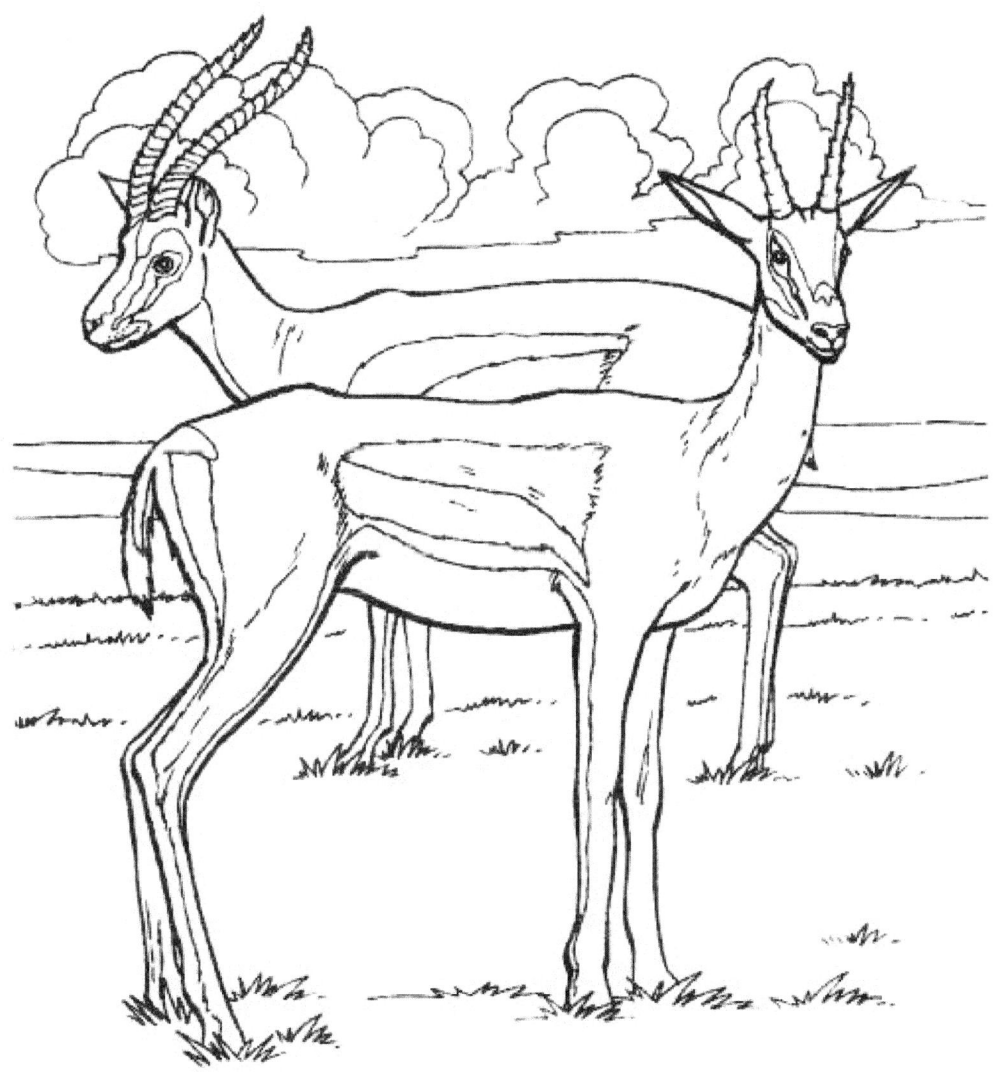

Gazelles

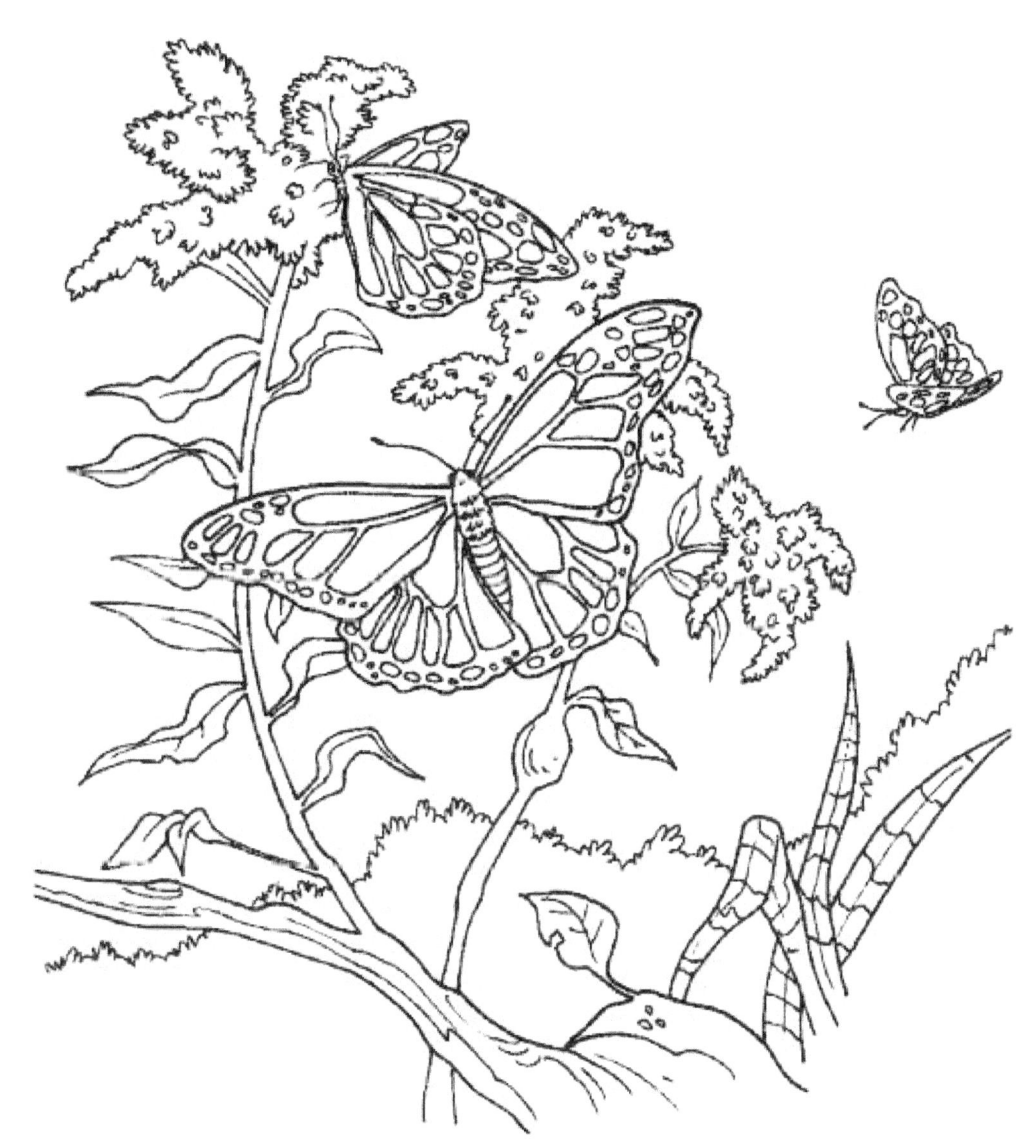

Butterflies

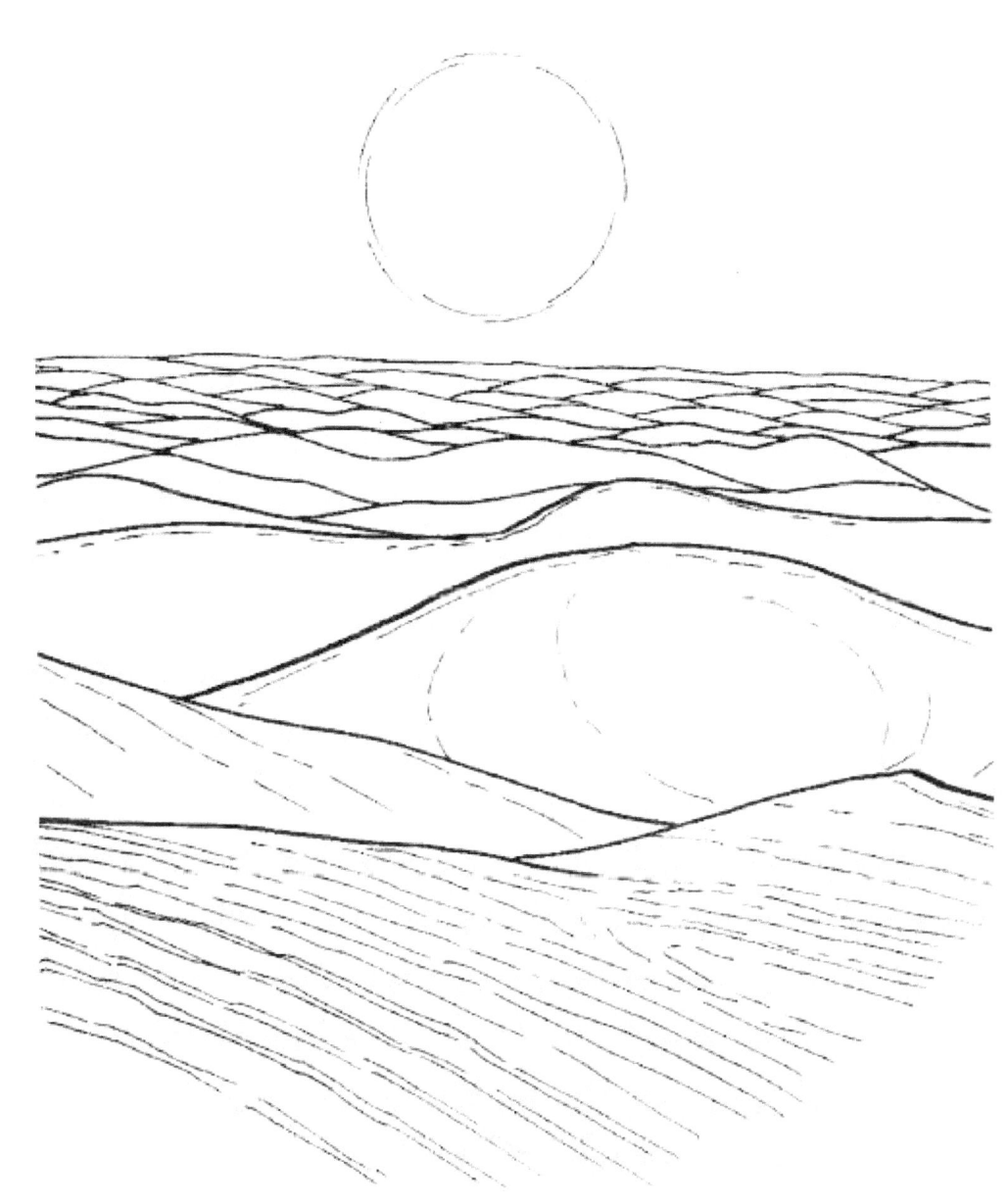

Sand Dunes

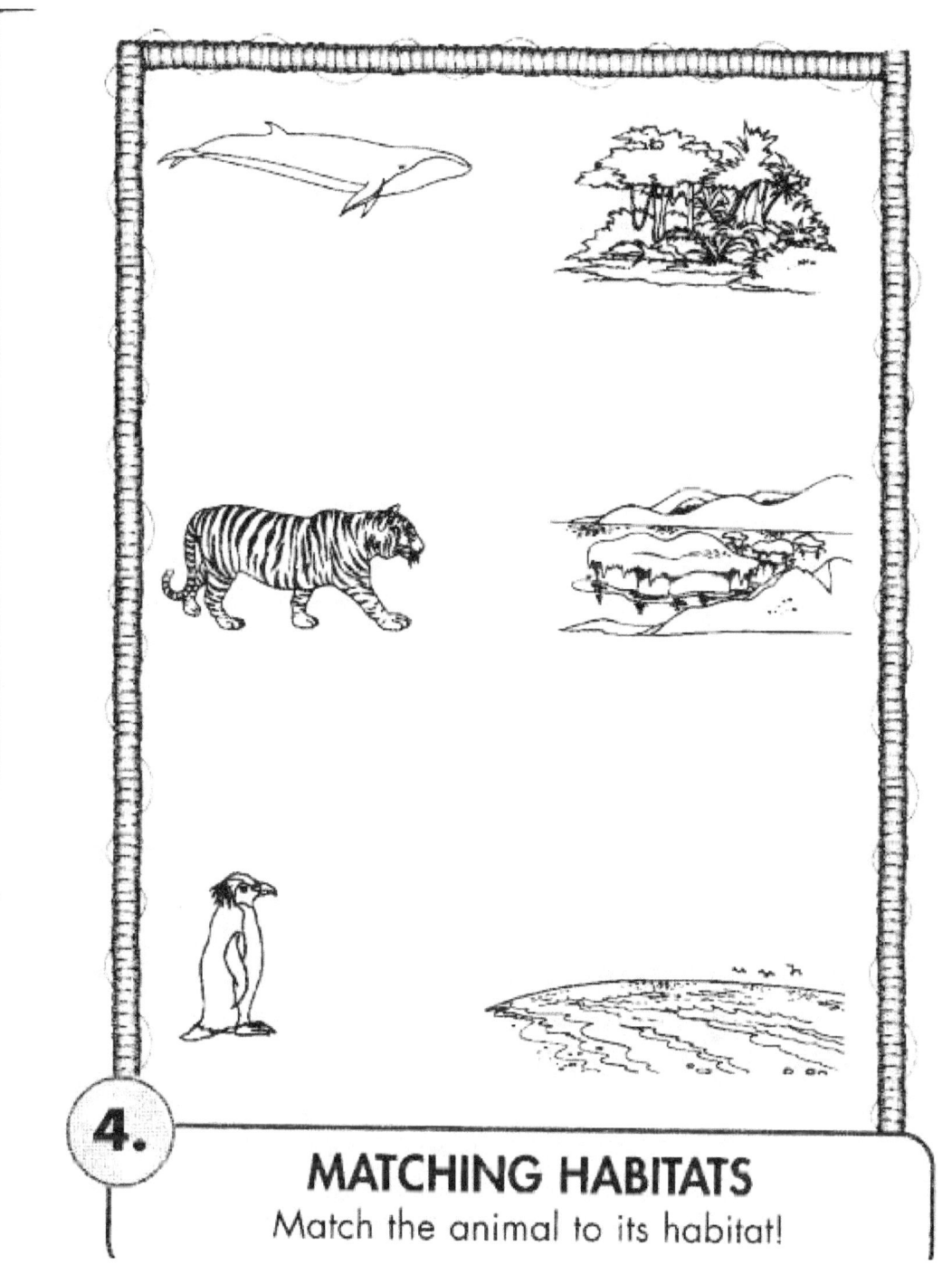

MATCHING HABITATS
Match the animal to its habitat!

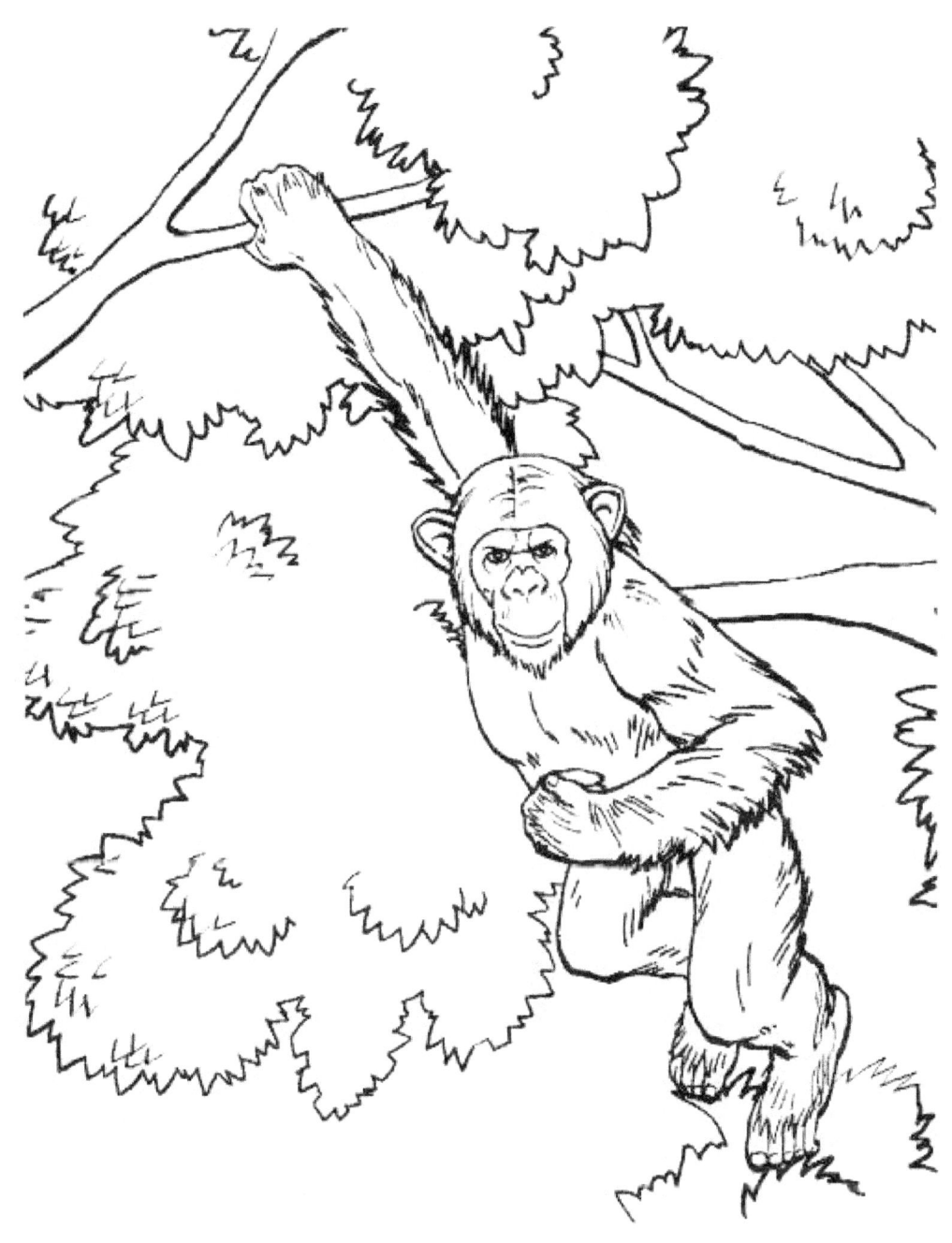

Chimpanzee

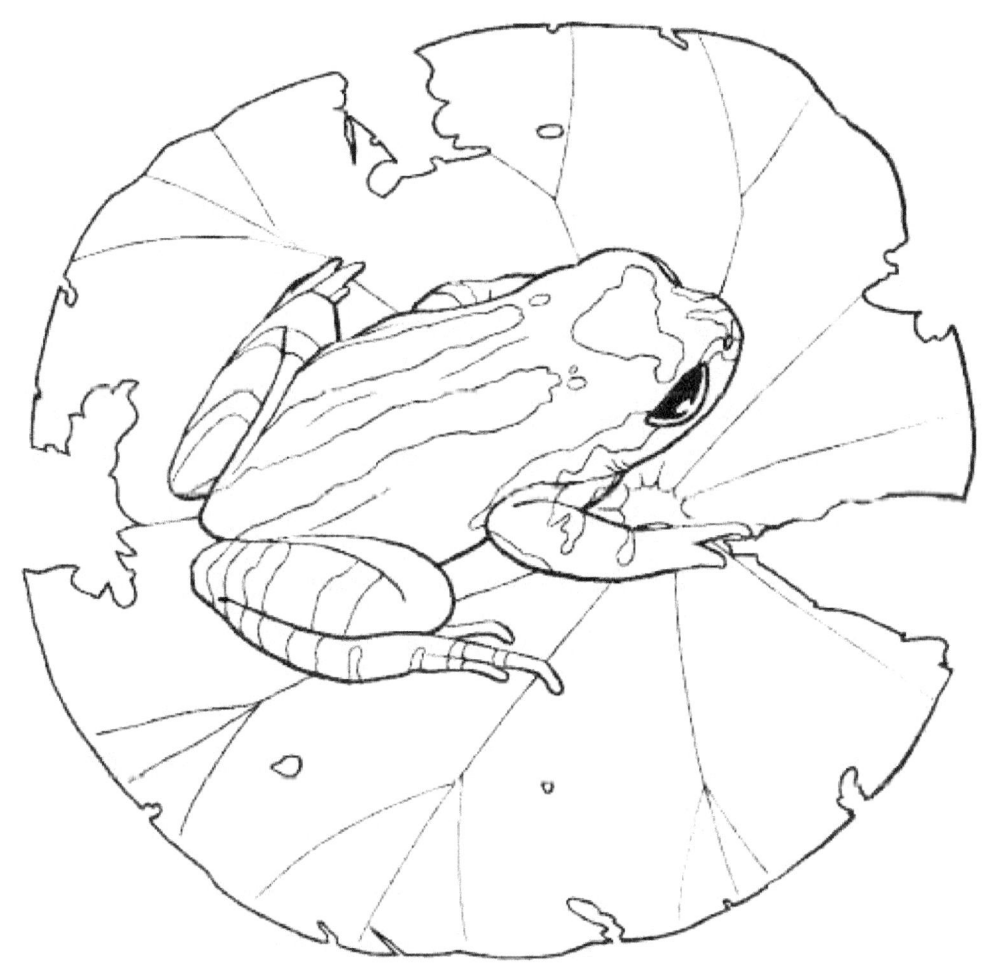

Frog

www.ingramcontent.com/pod-product-compliance
Lightning Source LLC
Chambersburg PA
CBHW081639220526
45468CB00009B/2503